Praise for *These are not the potatoes of my youth*

"The word 'queer' casts many shadows. Odd. Funny. Uncanny. Baffling. Matthew Walsh teases out what's queer about family, time, desire, and the self. An immense curiosity propels his explorations, unearthing scores of emotional and intellectual states. Wit sidles up to devotion. Vulnerability walks hand-in-hand with doubt."
 — Eduardo C. Corral, author of *Slow Lightning*

"Matthew Walsh dares readers to enter an urban world in which queer rurality is important, creative, poetic, and crucially disruptive to the norms of urban queer life. If the 'here' of this book isn't yours, then get ready. If it is, then wait no longer for a book that captures the impossible queerness of the Maritimes and its effect on more arrogant locales."
 — Lucas Crawford, author of *The High Line Scavenger Hunt*

MATTHEW WALSH

*These are not the potatoes
of my youth*

icehouse poetry

Copyright © 2019 by Matthew Walsh.

All rights reserved. No part of this work may be reproduced or used in any form or by any means, electronic or mechanical, including photocopying, recording, or any retrieval system, without the prior written permission of the publisher or a licence from the Canadian Copyright Licensing Agency (Access Copyright). To contact Access Copyright, visit www.accesscopyright.ca or call 1-800-893-5777.

Edited by Sheryda Warrener.
Cover and page design by Julie Scriver.
Cover illustration adapted from a work by lorasutyagina, 123RF Stock Photo.
Printed in Canada.
10 9 8 7 6 5 4 3 2 1

Library and Archives Canada Cataloguing in Publication

Walsh, Matthew, 1982-, author
    These are not the potatoes of my youth / Matthew Walsh.

Poems.
ISBN 978-1-77310-073-9 (softcover)

    I. Title.

PS8645.A4747T54 2019   C811'.6   C2018-904644-9

Goose Lane Editions acknowledges the generous financial support of the Government of Canada, the Canada Council for the Arts, and the Province of New Brunswick.

Goose Lane Editions
500 Beaverbrook Court, Suite 330
Fredericton, New Brunswick
CANADA E3B 5X4
www.gooselane.com

For all my friends who are family.

Poets, like potatoes, ripen in the dirt.
— Suzanne Buffam, *A Pillow Book*

Contents

11　Downtown convos
13　Purple haze
14　I'm bald
15　Potato life
16　From the prairies to the ocean is a long way to go
18　Sleeping outside the Kelowna bus station
19　Flaneurial
21　Nadine is good
23　Amanda
24　Agricola Street
27　Individual cats
30　Mushaboom
31　Speech impediment
33　Cringer
35　Garbage box with black loons
37　Your mother underground in St. Clair Station
39　Catholic and church
41　Mom types
42　Princess of Power
44　Airplanes to see your father
46　I think my dad liked me
47　Smile if your dad is like Orpheus
48　Blue potato
50　Wheelbarrow and cabbage
51　Red paprika
52　Sea glass
54　Cargo memories
56　View-Master
58　Maurice
59　George

60	Tool shed
61	The poem says
62	Contemporary
64	Couch potato
65	Kiss a horse
66	Tree of Mars
67	Seussians
68	Moonshot
69	Why I like baseball fields
70	Your dad's a regular guy
71	Dad with tomato plants
72	Potato people
73	Potatoes in my life
75	Inheritance and one ghost
77	Life of Bryan
79	More details forthcoming
81	The men in my family never talk about Alberta
83	Live-in boyfriend
85	If your dad is like Homer
87	For my future wilderness

Downtown convos

I thought someone was yelling *God bless, God bless*
after my walk through the fields of the Van Gogh exhibit
but a closer inspection told me they were just yelling *Columbus,
Columbus* to a pigeon I did not know
and upon even closer scrutiny they were just yelling
you missed it, you missed it.

I love to walk — it helps me see better the world, to be moving,
see what people are about and what they are doing
just saying hello, wow, taking my ear-
buds out, interacting, and I have made so many mistakes.

I let a guy once come on my eyes
because I didn't know what was happening, I thought
wow this is really low tide.

Because I was blessed
by a priest on his deathbed at the Grace Memorial
I take bigger chances, and I feel sometimes that Father
follows me and probably haunts me like fathers.

Once at a bathhouse I was offered four hundred dollars to perform
bareback but that would have covered barely
the cost of preventative medicine which acts
to kill your body. I have been here too long to stop
interior-decorating this body which has had so many show-
off moments and greens and vegetables.

In Vancouver I did love the love
letters and graffiti everywhere; people know how to live.
I loved taking a seat in the Chinese Classical Gardens
and I love to sip water dream and hear the snapping turtles
come up for air and I hear

they are aggressive lovers and I just want that
feeling of good loneliness for a while.
I keep walking because did I tell you no one believed in me
as a walker no one believed that I would walk until I did.

I walk past Hastings, Hastings Dance in complete ignorance
of traffic or danger, just to walk meadows of graffiti, and pass away
time in community gardens, where plants reveal their oldest art.
I met kale, zucchini, keeping people related to the dirt.

Purple haze

I had no idea that blackberry bushes could grow up
into trees. I might be high
but these guys leave
big black holes at my feet. I wish life was more
cartoony and I could climb down through
like a coyote but it is just a sidewalk stain.

And it's ok. In gardens pulled weeds lie
in the position of the old pastoral, dark yellows, burnt umber
and it is a golden light.

And Science World is a giant blueberry tonight.
And I find myself again walking backwards like on rewind
to Gastown and the old steam clock
everyone waits to hear from and I love the orange
cranes on the waterfront like little horses
or giraffes. Maybe you see what I mean.

At night the neon city workers from the road sector
inspecting all the manholes are marked XXX
as one lifts up the covering so they can all peer down
into what I can only imagine is the pupil of the road.

I'm bald

At first, I thought it was Seymour in Vancouver
but it was the Mount Royal that I was climbing,
with discarded T-shirts, condoms, and fast food wrappers so reminiscent
of my baby-gay self's bedroom floor.

If fast food can find itself here then I will not
be the David of this mountain.

There is an old apostle running down the staircase, from above
he may resemble a grain of sand falling through Escher's hour-
glass. He is training the excesses of his heart
and that is something that I have done with the veneer of dedication.

At this age, we may begin to imagine what death might be like.
I predict I will fall beautifully in the shower singing Céline Dion
and on top, overlooking the city, how it pumps like an organ
confirming that it sustains life.

There are so many signs and lifetime warranties, the golden arches
with billions and billions served and I heard from a nurse
who cared for more than literature that we should not reminisce on the silly
things we wanted. I have found the glasses on my head.

Death is the point where we fall
silent to the entanglement of our tongue and I want to go
out screaming and laughing like a Blue Jays
fan. If I return to my Patricia Hotel I can certainly make it
out on the train, knowing no one
will comb my hair on a mountain.

Potato life

My friend is having such a hard time getting potatoes to grow.
The time for heroic patience is over. I'm a descendant
of farmers and I don't know. It is like her light beam has gone out.
The plot is ready. I had said I would hoe it real good but forgot —
maybe I don't want to be reminded of the potato's connective tissue.
She is concerned they may be too inhibited,
bought egg cartons to root them,
but I said put them in the closet with the printer,
and yet nothing is working.
Maybe seeing them reach out will cause screaming.
Once I swam the length of my grandfather's potato garden,
which went underappreciated —
what the hell was I doing out there — the dog-paddle, the butterfly?
I thought I was a dog.
The sun had seriously come out, his potatoes were doing so well.
Some had blue skins, yet they breathed.
What he did was talk potato which my friend was not going to do.
She threw them out of the house for the night.

In a museum as a kid not yet covered in dirt, I saw little potato-
head dolls, so precious, untouched behind glass.
Dolls unlike my Peaches 'n Cream Barbie
which was begged for, with real down-home charm.
How long had the potatoes been heads?
Nearly a hundred years. My friend thinks *doom*
for the root vegetables. I think my head should be in a museum,
there have been ten chances at least — she had been reaching out for weeks.

From the prairies to the ocean is a long way to go

In Slave Lake, Alberta, I fell in love with a stationery man
who worked the projector nights at the single-

screen theatre. His family a stationery family, his mother
a stationery mother who painted *Still Life with Greyhound*

and Fruits. His family in Red Deer Pulp and Paper.
They were not sick of it — paper was their blood.

My first time in Drumheller I was like *what the hell
is this place*. I slept on old slaughterhouse land. I had fucked-up

dreams where I told upset cows I loved cows
pulled cherries on the VLT where in the motel bathroom

perhaps a cow wrote *how do you tell up from down*
but there were no answers.

More south there were green lizards on blazing hot ground, famous
with locals and a Nevada couple who wasted themselves

of their international data plan on him. Big mistake, Nevadans,
but in the moment things seem worth it.

I got cold sleeping in a car dealership under a comforter
of a 2002 Sedan Ultima, in Brandon took pictures of Brandon

University for a friend of a friend, Brandon, got my palm read through
Thunder Bay by Sharon who talked me through the surrounding areas.

I like to watch the world pass on the highway, deer
at night their ears like satellites, and houses that added something

to the urban sprawl and Dear, Toronto I heard you were dating
a man who was me but not like me which is fine for me

to still be where I want. I fell asleep in Quebec near Valentine's Day
and woke up in Cap-de-la-Madeline where I met La Bonhomme.

People threw maple syrup on snow and things were simple and old
with fiddles and a man who followed me through the city

and I agreed *yes, Banff is a catalogue city*, of course, and I was tired
of the air conditioner breathing on me like a drunk guy

and where I missed the cadence of my legs where
all my bony landmarks were sore and I wasn't 30,000 feet in the air

on the edge of a mountain and thinking maybe I could fly,
maybe I could fly all the way down.

Sleeping outside the Kelowna bus station

I woke to a small brown rabbit behind a blade
of grass. He was completely confused.

Shouldn't I be making pancakes on the moon? Did I not
have another place to be? But I had not gone

and his friends looked at me like I was a person
who would just invite himself

to their party. My grandfather hated rabbits
but I didn't share that with him.

I tried to sleep but I felt his whiskers on my face.
I had never kissed a rabbit before.

My grandmother once ate rabbit brains
fried in Becel with thirty percent less salt.

I prayed this would not come up. How could
I rationalize that? I wanted to hold him so badly.

He had been sweet to me though belonged elsewhere
with someone else. He licked water

from grass and his friends were so great. I'd get him
a ticket in the morning to come with me

but he could not leave. He was the only one
who could get the TV to come in.

He knew I had to return to the moon. He had no time
or love, for I was a space cadet.

Flaneurial

I can walk into the Red Sea
Café through the predictable pop of "Call Me
Maybe." I just passed a sign that said *Leave Male
for Spider Holding* and I tried leaving,

I digested it, walking towards the Lite-
On Computers, Broadway St., Vancouver to the web
of transit. Destination, Terminal Avenue.

I tell myself to pick up where others left off in the sudoku
and eat a green emerald

curry. What about my insides did you feel you owned
enough to go secretly unprotected with the men of the art world
and not tell me how far your artistry had gone.

When we saw the Kandinsky in Montreal you found it
not nourishing? Asked *where the hell is he in painting?*

Maybe a genius, but definitely dead. I felt invited in, his blobs
were everything. Spheres, maybe planets in isolated cold space.
Several Circles, 1926 described as romantic?

And the same purple circle in *Gravitation*? You feel he is starving.
Oh, blue rider, he makes the sun melt all of Moscow.

Things became more abstract as we moved along, who cares,
so what, you appreciated his doctor's office aesthetic
and said I needed one when I could definitely taste the red?

When I landed my life in Vancouver I got told the mountain range
was called Sleeping Beauty by the descendant of a Russian oligarch

but all I saw was my own perspectives: the ears of a very mad dog,
the molars, more earth, head of a canine. So how are you,
my puppy guy?

We have different eyes. I am in these mountains which are so far out
from the corner of Milky Way and Queen where you rest
in your own atmosphere, and we have different brains

and yesterday I saw a whole school
of cyclists like little neon fish
and one swam past the red light, past a Sunset
Food delivery truck getting to the other side.
People do stupid things all the time. Yesterday I read
with Girl in a Wetsuit while she looked at the sea

and she is on a different plane than me, and there was so much yesterday
I found a *fortune* on the pavement: two days from now tomorrow
will be yesterday.

On the bus for the first time I saw a man open up
a container of grapes like it was the last sweet thing he would taste,
the last Earth grape.

Nadine is good

I took pictures of her black eye with a Konica camera
so the police would finally see
her partner. She would grab my throat
to feel my lymph nodes when she lived

with us and read them, trying to figure out who I was
in a past life. And she would cut red beets

and make borscht for my lymph nodes, and I was worried
about her — she was like my grandmother with a crew-
cut dating a terrible man who wore only sailor costumes.

Red borscht, carrot soup: they are good roots. She left
always something stewing on low.

Nadine played a hand drum every evening to ease tensions
between the day and night, a very hard transition personally for her.

She was interested in my neck and called it Walt Whitman
when we watched TV or stepped out for Du Mauriers.

I confessed to her my fear of the future and she was annoyed,
read my tarot cards constantly because I was selfish
but loved magic and wanted to know what she knew about life

and I would find out, certainly. The root of my tongue
she found and the boiling water I would pour for her
and stare deep into the black holes of her nostrils

as she put her hands on my neck, feeling my lymph nodes,
whispering *Walt Whitman, Walt Whitman*
and I think I started speaking up for myself then

she was late for dinner, said she could not get past
an energy field but did we believe her?

She brought around John who hit
on me once in the downstairs bathroom, he wanted
to suck my dick but I was not ready for the abuse

of intimacy. When Nadine left, my friend said she was gone
clearing blockages in rivers but we didn't know where

she was. We wanted to check rivers for any blockages
she had fixed. I wanted to feel her hands

around my neck, Walt Whitman, but she turned up
after Hurricane Juan, in the *Chronicle Herald*

helping people get warm, to cook meat and soup
around this giant fire so much like that energy field.

Amanda

She can turn you into a pretzel. Spent two thousand and one
repeating the mantra *bony landmarks bony landmarks*

and listening to Clipse music. She once turned five dollars into strawberries
and a two-litre Baxter ice cream. So supportive — I thought I could grow

old in her spare room. Once we changed a man into a horse
and into a man again. Once I dated a giant

who broke our pull-out Japanese cedar futon from the internet
and my bed and the internet and we can laugh

about it now. Amanda is an essential
oil master. She told me that my aura was blue with red freckles

and would ask me sometimes to let go
of my body so she could turn me into a pretzel. I was scared

to be a pretzel but she was a great re-arranger. I had parts
of myself I did not know were part of myself.

My little pea-shaped bone adjacent to the clavicle sounded
beautiful and cracked beautifully. She thought my problem

was I could not imagine my body as spaghetti
through guided imagery. At restaurants she could never decide,

did she want cedar plank roasted salmon or the Thai long noodle
soup. She found for me my greater trochanter.

I couldn't shut up about it, she located my wing
of ilium and said now I could let go of my legs.

Agricola Street

We had our house cleaned by Margie
and Doug, who went through our house feeling

the walls. It was a sensitive time for the house.
We had just moved in.

The blue wall in my room was puffy
and Amanda left

music on all night, for comfort I think. There were no words,
just instruments. Creaking. Those things.

Her friend had come from the other side
of town and airbrushed butterflies on her stomach

that Amanda called very pregnant. Sometimes we slept
together with the ghetto blaster pulled in close

and listened to Modest Mouse or talk
radio. We would listen to it talking.

Amanda was the most sensitive
to the house's conversation. She understood

a hundred percent of it. Margie brought nothing
with them except sage

and a bag of salt
for sprinkling. I liked its earthy smell, green,

with leaves,
it had been a member of the Four Thieves

Vinegar, an elixir for the plague. Margie liked the house
plants because they breathed out and in

oxygen. There was space to breathe. The last I had seen Doug
and Margie they were dressed as Klingons

at the Halifax Comic Con. They called themselves Nitrast
Kroch and Edras Tizect. They had to cross

the American border every six months
but not with their alien names. Doug was American

and always leaving their home on the cheapest flights
for the reclining airplane seats, small TV trays

to keep his citizenship, their life. We wanted to leave
our house, cut our losses. Nothing could grow here.

We slept in the living room
it was the place with the most light.

This world is nuts, Doug said. Coming from the state
of Wisconsin where it appears flat with one plane,

all dirt, and all of these rules of where you have to be
and why. He felt haunted by immigration.

My father did not know how to set boundaries with spirits;
they seemed to just follow him. He never saw

anything, ectoplasm, doors opening.
Just sounds of running, a light he remembered

turning off. I became mum about it — didn't like feeling haunted
and I wasn't the expert on other people's ghosts.

I just heard a crackling sound
someone secretly opening a bag of Hostess potato

chips, bad television reception. Amanda,
she would ask, *Do you hear that?*

We sat with the living
room furniture and listened to the rocking

chair's own opinions and struggles. It was kind
of intangible. It was hard to say

what it meant. I broke
the silence saying I'd never used sage in

cooking. We lit the sage on the burner, stood in the closet
and moved slowly through the house

like we were seasoning it
for a good winter of staying together, a clean space.

Individual cats

I recommend the Superstore parking lot, deep December,
for coming out. Your mother will look like she is smoking

but not smoking, just doing her best
bull impression. Two bags in each hand like a scale

of justice or a Libra emoji. She changes topic quick,
is excited for her trip to Cuba, she hopes it's all nuts

down there, and hot. She was so excited for it
because goats were like people's cats in Cuba

and that is what she likes: real life. We stopped for clementines,
the quintessential Christmas fruit.

We were such tourists as she walked me down the aisle. It felt good
to live life. She looked for fruit for the fruitcake;

it was all so laughable because I knew what was coming for good
in just a few minutes. Hopefully a *do you remember a time thing*,

a long drive to Musquodoboit by way of Mushaboom. My mom loves
to keep clementines in the closet to ripen up which is so good

in a poem I am making over. We came out together
from the Superstore and I turned and said *I am gay*

which was scary comical 'cause she had so much fruit
on her hands, now, literally, for real.

I suppose all the times dressing as a woman
for Halloween now seemed so wrong, helping me

put an old bra on, my insistence to wear her pink lip-
stick. When I was born the apartment upstairs had ideas

my mother had a Siamese cat, stereotypically whiny cats,
but it was me who cried all night possibly

knowing this day would come and worried that I couldn't say
it. When the apartment complained her favourite saying was born:

get your head out of your ass. Her son was not a cat. Get your head
out of the tabloids: *Mother Gives Birth to Creature Wearing Women's Fashion.*

Once I had a friend who said my fingernails were too long
for a boy but how should a boy be? What a constant battle, especially

in the '80s, in kindergarten when I wanted my name to be pink
not blue. But my mom is so good about everything now:

she says when you're in a new place you have to make friends.
I tell her sometimes I want my friend to come

home and catch me singing to the cat songs about him being a baby
cat. And Amanda was not my lover but my spiritual advisor.

My mother still returns to the produce section, she loves her little oranges,
I know that. I wonder if she remembers

taking me to see Woody the Talking Christmas Tree,
the tree who may yet still wear more garlands than Judy

Garland. I wonder if she thinks about the first time I saw her
after coming out where she stuffed my bed with HIV

pamphlets which scared me, but she was a nurse from the '80s
and had seen what could happen, and I try to remember

where she is coming from, when I still wind around her ankles,
and show her that behaviour of cats varies dramatically.

Mushaboom

There are Polaroids found of my mother,
with acoustic guitars, in the kitchen
by the rotary phone big as the modern day
house cat. Her grandfather, Alex, came over in the belly
of a boat with only Gaelic, a violin, fiddle, and maybe dreams
I don't know — but I know they were in the past
musical. I would like to know what happened.
Like, why no more music. And these parties, legendary
things would happen — people burned holes in spoons
playing the spoons. The violin when I was young,
oh I saw it, but was told I did not have the chin.

My great-grandfather, Alex, was, I believe, a giant,
three steps and he'd be in the depths
of the Atlantic and soon returning home with little fish.
I remember sitting next to him on the chesterfield,
he would stare straight out the picture
window at the road. I tried to speak in fiddle
but my mother just worried I was too cat.

There was a green cassette tape with uncles singing
very scratchy sounds in 1987 when Rita MacNeil
was Nova Scotia's answer to The Beatles, a picture
of Uncle Cyril, little inscription: *Cyril,
died in war, beautiful singing voice, Mushaboom, 1941.*

It seemed like art, to play an instrument.
There were rumours our grandfather played with Snow,
Hank Snow at the Legion Hall, but he passed
up the chance, kept doing the Sunday Legion dances
which made no sense. He did not want to
travel anymore, my mother said, and I wanted to
know what legendary things no one can remember.

Speech impediment

At a party my mother got so drunk on Bacardi Breezers she revealed
that I had been deprived

of oxygen for five minutes or something. I sat there dumbfounded.
That is why your leg is lame a little. And why your brain is different.

Apparently, I was not expected to be able to walk. Well, now I walk
all over the face of the Earth sometimes with dog poop on my soles.

When I told an ex-boyfriend this he said my mother should not be able
to reproduce but I like my brain.

And my brother had his own language.
He did therapy and gained confidence. I saw him clearly,

once, re-enacting the final scene from *The Lion King* as Simba
on his hands and knees, roaring *before* Katy Perry

which was also the same day he drank Drano, thinking oooh Blue
Raspberry Kool-Aid.

I don't feel the pressure to be smart all the time. In kindergarten
my class was given baby chickens

we were to watch grow,
but they remained eggs. Power had left the school

and to our new brains we did not understand a towel
over the incubator. Mrs. Gardener quickly explained the twenty-six deaths

it just comes so suddenly which terrified everyone completely.
When we swam I put a towel over my brother. He was a little star

of the IWK TV Telethon. He had an open heart
surgery at one. He was supposed to have a role as a survivor

but got diarrhea. Now he is a crane
operator and still has trouble with esses. This was certainly sad

but now he does public speaking and we watch spaghetti westerns
for the delay. We car tripped to the mouth of the Madawaska,

home of aerospace and human innovation. My brother, chain smoking
out the window of a white Toyota he had bought himself that summer.

Cringer

I've based my entire masculinity on He-Man
Master of the Universe's green pet tiger,
Cringer. He had such a good character,
and I wore a mask like him, I breathed
in medicines for my lungs, for bronchitis.
My mother messed up my tiger hair, called
me Cringer. Dad had sort of closed the door
to me, for I was not athletic, like he. Cringer
was shy but in his mask he became confident.
Like a boy in my class, Graeme.
I was born with a weakness and addicted
to cigarettes. I knew I liked boys
more than most girls which was a depravity.
I loved running after them, though I was not built for
chasing. I dragged my leg a bit through the drug-
stores waiting for my prescription which
came in big brown bottles like liquor, tasted
like window cleaner. In the cartoon, Cringer
was an embarrassment, though a prophecy
said he was not what he seemed to be. My mother
slipped the mask over my head, told me to just breathe
in while I dreamed of living in the woods
with Graeme, building a dream house, blending
shyness with my outgoingness. I jumped
at everything, the possible dangers, a blanket
with a chair under it. After breathing
in my medicines I made salad from weeds
in the driveway. Dandelion flowers, blue gravel
where I imagined blueberry. I was young, hungry
for more than salad but had no language
for it. I went to Graeme's birthday, sank
his ships with dimes in the bathtub, so excited

that I closed my airway temporarily. I was not
the most powerful man in the universe,
and not entirely what I seemed to be just now.

Garbage box with black loons

My father's speech was slurred most of my childhood — but it's a rite
of passage for many Maritime Canadians
'cause I heard from a friend of a friend that linguists say our accent
is the result of a speech impediment, yet I don't think much
of it. My father comes from people who learned to talk
the potato into growing more potatoes — a trick
not a lot of people know.
And people who cottage here think life is very easy
and carefree. The potato money bought
groceries and the rest went towards my father's brand new
two-door red Toyota Tercel
the closest thing we could afford to a Lamborghini
and the most practical vehicle for a middle-aged man with four kids
who now would get very creative
with cans of tuna, white bread, and chicken legs with veins, bought in bulk,
which Shake 'n Bake: The Original could not fix.
All summer, chicken legs with veins
and hairy legs and Dad daydreaming his
two-door Toyota Tercel was sports
car material and so on weekends he found himself
whatever he could to make himself garbage
boxes, and they would sell, oh yes, everyone wanted a box
for all the garbage they dealt with, totally
beautiful at the end of their cottage driveways
next to the Anne of Green Gables mailbox
hand-painted by a local artist, my third-grade teacher.
Have Dad's blood in my veins, despite my early convictions
that we were not related and that Dad may also
be a tourist of this town for he felt like he belonged
elsewhere. Because I cannot build garbage
boxes, I know nothing about the art, the discipline
of carpentry, or raising a shed which he also did

from the scraps of his childhood house torn down
when land was sold to tourists who loved quaint life
and it paid for the car and there were no more veins
in the chicken and we had a garbage box, and a shed,
built from his own house, a shed he painted
and named Cow, and he loved putting up
any kind of wall, and this he can do just from scratch
like driving his red car looking at junk and making it
into something strangers would love him for.

Your mother underground in St. Clair Station

In St. Clair station, you seem to be growing
tired of waiting for the woman who pointed to your first rainbow.
She pulled off road, to the edge of the Atlantic and said, *there, there
look up, your first rainbow*. And you marvelled
she knew something so magical.

As a kid it was not science, but magic. Not beams of light reflected
through water, but actual real colours. When you grew
distant she treaded water at the YWCA, waiting

for a moment in your life when you would just be ok.
When you were born, she worried about your addiction
to cigarettes — she could not give it up, she loved to blow smoke
out her nose at barbecues. She loved to yell at anyone
you do not know what it is like to create a life from scratch.

You remember bringing your first boyfriend home from scratch,
a three-hundred-pound giant you looked up to, she got fried
eggs and bacon ready, fresh towels, like hotel guests receive,
possibly a nervous reflex for the gay aspects in her life she grappled
with, but now she has given up the habit of worrying about your health.

When you call, she says don't worry, she is with the doctors.
They are infatuated with her, say they need her
tissues when they talk about what future
and all she wants is to sit and plant herself
flowers. They may need to put a little needle in her brain,
to explore the ellipses of little black dots on her X-ray
but sometimes she just wants to sit in the grass and dream
sometimes. She wants to walk along the ocean that creeps
closer every year to her house, you barely notice it, she says.

The doctors say she might have had a little stroke yet not
known it. Nothing is clear aside from the entrance
to the metro where you wait for her, where you picture her
looking out the kitchen window at the ocean, hands covered in Magic
Baking Powder, hands spent
nursing, where you hope you have to explain the transit
system and become annoyed at her Window Shopping as Cardio
work-out routine. You want her to fall down
and watch *The Kids in the Hall* on your fat Toshiba,
this is supposed to be her vacation time, watching the *Wheel of Fortune*
reruns and she will come floating towards you,
down the escalator. She might, but she might not.

Catholic and church

It would have made things easier if at an earlier age I could have said
the word *gender* but I grew up in a place where no one talked

dirty or questioned. We would go through the clothes and suitcases,
fight over the tea cups of dead relatives and donate

to the church and I never ever got anything back but being held back
in Sunday school one year, what, because I wasn't a good enough human

or something? And I can't eat any more of his body, or those wafers
they taste like a body. I feel like a man's body

makes me feel nothing when I have no choice. Church no longer means man
and woman under God to me.

No, it does not — it is a street in Toronto
where you find out having the best time of your life that Mariah Carey

is now considered retro and you stand there
in the middle of the dance floor, ghost of your former baby-gay self

in Bluenotes jeans and your Bluenotes Motion T-shirt with brown leaves
and your neck covered in blueberry hickeys, that you are *middle-aged.*

Church St. is the mother ship and it called me back and said
I am so glad you didn't end up a priest Jesus fucking Christ — no it didn't

say that but it is the first place I felt masculinity was not rewarded
and handed a trophy or was listening at the door to your in-person

interview and wanted to ruin you. Church is the place
to go when I'm sad to just walk around and everyone knows sadness while

they sit smoking outside your body after a drag number to Whitney
and you sit there with cheese fries, gravy on the side, totally stunned

by this stranger who does not share any relation to you. You sit there
screaming on the inside *how do you know my inner life*

how do you know my innards and Jada Hudson's wig blessed me
when her hair brushed my face but it was with the greatest love of all.

Mom types

I swear my mom is just one of those regular mom types who has eyes
on the back of her head. Her husband left her on New Year's Eve —
not kidding. It was perfect timing. It just so happened most wives
in the area were changing
the locks on their homes so their husbands, I assume, would return
to the forest. She savours now the full-time loneliness of just being
one of those Maritime divorcees, big on bingo and trying
to see if chances come in seconds like dinner. She has all my childhood
drawings and moments stored away
and they come out sometimes when she has too many Labatt Blues.

My mother is like any mother — knows when the salmon are running
just by looking at the ocean. She has healing powers
which I believe came from drinking so much
Pepsi. She is a Pisces but more crab-like, left arm stronger
than its twin from pulling gold, pulling cherries on the VLT.

She still has all her dresses from the '80s, it's magical
because teal and lace are never seen together in nature.
I love her fantasy, her drunk *Guitar Hero* and real guitar
capabilities. She comes from a line of musicians
and a grandfather who once played fiddle for Snow —
Hank Snow but that could be rumours.

Her hair is silver, yet she still does midnight Zumba,
has seen so much in terms of deaths, figurative and literal.
She is something like a phenomenon,
yet so little, and describes herself as the last thing people see
before they die. She is so grim and not an angel
of death. She has done so much and I don't
know everything about her, yet when I look
in her closet I see my entire life.

Princess of Power

I have no idea what Catholic manliness is, that kind of manliness
seems so boring I'm sorry most of my family

who are dead and will haunt me now. Are you really not able to talk
about most things, be so stern in always having to wear pants

if you are a boy? Please no — it sounds like a horror story.
I never want to nail up all the gyprock in one afternoon drunk

on Labatt Blue. These rituals are weird and I will not partake.
And only drinking rum out of a 42-ounce *Jurassic Park* glass

from McDonalds? Don't bother explaining — I'm out catching eels
until dinner and yes, I am letting them all go.

I am tired of all my naked baby photos still in circulation and why during
card games did I have to lie naked on brown two-dollar bills with robins

on them, or if I was lucky, a five-dollar bill with my favourite bird of all,
the blue jay. I'm sure now why I have a complex. It is not from dancing wrong

at a high school MuchMusic video dance party with a former babysitter.
I didn't know my hands went on her waist; it just seems wrong

still to make anyone do that. I think being Catholic made everything
totally weird. No one in my family likes being told what to do;

it was all peer pressure. And why the peeled potatoes in silver bowls,
and why so much ham, and kneeling? Why the final declaration in

the Bible, No Neon Sweatpants in Church? Oh, I did not believe strongly
in God in the Clouds. You know what I planned to do? Eat communion wafers

in church before being confirmed. And why does he speak
to only a chosen few? Come off it. I am going to put a dress on

a Christmas tree. And I couldn't be a priest. I did not want to wait
at the end of people's driveways on Christmas Eve.

My only true and real idols told me not to take priesthood
seriously, I am the child of He-Man and She-Ra, Princess of Power.

Airplanes to see your father

I feel like airplanes are where memories are stored —
no, that's wrong — I don't; I'm just trying to begin this process
of a poem. I FaceTimed into his hospital room, outside visiting hours,
and he is all dressed in white bedsheets.
This is as close as I can get. I am trying to remember anything
I remember about him, the back of his head, driving
from field

of baseball to field of baseball. I'm sitting there disoriented
from my personal nest. I have the brain
of a small bird.

He wants to give me his coin collection, kept sacredly
in his Blue Raspberry Kool-Aid tin, another collection
of Kinder Surprise toys — little animals and vehicles, special editions.
My mother texts, *are you collecting or not?*

I don't really know too much about him. The sky changes
blue to pink like my old Hyper-Colour T-shirt from the Sears Catalogue
which disappeared when it stayed pink.

I can't believe we live in a world where colours have been gendered.
Up here, over... *Wyoming?* Clouds look like brains, giant thinking palaces.
I'm sorry but the you in the poem needs to relax.

He never liked it when I drug my leg through Lawton's Drugs
I'm sorry I feel lame. I'm just a passenger in this body

I feel has never fit me. The snow-capped mountains remind me
of my father's cataracts and the sun is mortal
and your father is mortal. I have a tiny window

to look over the fields, tiny squares of farmland remind me
of my father's patchwork quilt, such a tiny window.

As he pulls it up over his legs in the gentle glow
of the television. From far above I see channels
of rivers, flowers of highways, many flowers, freeways and all that,
and the descent, fragments of land and all that.

I think my dad liked me

I think my dad liked me because he once called me
lover.

I think my dad liked me because he never saw me
dance, swivel-hipped, my arms careless around Andrea's shoulders.

I think my dad liked me because I loved my baseball glove
with the blue jay on the palm.

I think my dad liked me because I was good at pretending
I wanted a Pamela Anderson poster in my room.

I think my dad liked me because he didn't know what I wanted was to be
Pamela Anderson in the red bathing suit, circa *Baywatch* theme song credits.

I think my dad liked me because sometimes I stood in the darkness
scared to step into the light.

I think my dad liked me because he didn't know me
as the boy who chased boys with my mother's lipstick.

I think my dad liked me because Mrs. Gardener told him I was popular
with girls but it was for braiding hair.

I think my dad liked me because he didn't know another boy
asked why I wasn't a boy.

I think my dad liked me because I liked his baseball trophies
for the winged woman at the top.

I think my dad like me because I had actually built something
he didn't know about me.

Smile if your dad is like Orpheus

He says if you're gonna smile then don't
waste any time doing it. He, a late-blooming philosopher sitting

by the river — too strong, with dark water, totally impractical for children
to swim in. And yet he calls

the water-skipper a genius in theology
for the floating alone. He drinks Labatt Blue

from a cooler, yelling, *be a man, be brave*, while you stare
deeply at the river which looks like the black hair

of your mother who is nursing close to death
the elderly and the family of others, and not currently

present to say *maybe don't. You don't have to.* And he shows you
that he can swim the riverbed

and suddenly wow your rivals but you never needed to be
that masculine. You let him channel his inner amphibian

up to his brainstem, a floating head of metamorphosis,
and dive to where the water is mostly leeches, yet he recovers

your shoes that you were sure had died, an old vacuum, a '64 dime.
He is your father for a day

at the river, who leaves when the flowers close, when bees go
back to their honeycombs. He drinks, gargles

in the bathroom, his practice of ranges, vocals and your father floats
out, he's laughing that he's actually touched bottom.

Blue potato

Once during a harvest, we found a blue potato
and that was when I started to believe in life
on other planets. I had to be a seed from a plant no one knew

and now we were all doomed. This is what happens when you come
from a line of potato husbands. All the uncles and men wore hats

that hid the eyes. *Potatoes*, the uncles said, *good yield*.
They were so basic. Dad told me blue potatoes were magic

and now I can blame him for my overactive imagination
and wow were we ever rich
in the potato department. What I loved were the potato flowers
which I kept fresh in a drinking glass by the sink
under the impression it would live forever this way
in my captivity.

There were times I had to grub potatoes from the garden for dinner
and I would sit on the grass, thinking gardens were like swimming pools
because my logic was sound.

As a girl my grandmother used potato leaves to tell fortunes
to know what boy to marry
but when I asked what boy I would marry
she said no boy, a girl.

I wanted to be dropped into a metal bowl with water
and when I asked why she said *the potato leaves*
and I would just stare at this familiar large pile of dirt
wondering what life was under it and

when I lifted up rocks I would see all kinds of life
but the adults always had their eyes on the backs of their heads
watching me and I would leave
to make potato deliveries, or potato trades, potato salads
and dream of growing many eyes and owning
my own aisles of produce on another planet not this planet.

Wheelbarrow and cabbage

My grandfather used to lie about his profession.
He told me he was a schoolteacher in the math field.

In his garden he took attendance which I believed to be a habit
from his school days. He looked at what was there, counted
rows of pumpkin, the plot of cauliflower which did look like brains.

And cabbages so big he didn't even think he could move them based
on his weight times the age he had become. All his sons,

who could carry cabbages on their shoulders while grandfather
counted the heads, moved on. One September, he had too many of them —
if he did not harvest them under the Harvest Moon they would turn

into children from the moon. I did not want any more sisters or brothers.
But I would stand up for them if it came to it on the brutal playgrounds.

I would scream *he ain't a cabbage, he's my brother*. Who cares
if someone thinks you are a lunatic if you are doing what is right.
My grandfather would take a knife to them and cut them

from the ground, lifted them hardly into his wheelbarrow which fit six
and me comfortably. I liked riding with my family. In the house he scared me,

pretending he didn't know which was a cabbage and which was me.
I would try to convince him that he did not grow me. I was cabbage not.
Maybe a boy, or because shyness, tomato — half vegetable, half fruit.

Red paprika

In Italy my mother would be considered a criminal; luckily
we never had money to go there. You can be fined for boiling lobsters
alive in the country shaped like an elegant boot.
She knows three ways to kill and is ruthless.
She has a guy up shore who does the hard work.
He gives them to her in a ripping garbage bag
And she runs to the car, breathless — I have seen this
with my eyes. Once, the police stopped us
and she said *oh hello officer I am just trying to get my kid home
before dark*. It was two in the afternoon, a Sunday.
Complete. Duplicity.

She would get my grandmother involved, would call
and say *the eagle has landed*. My grandmother would appear
out of nowhere with a big, black speckled lobster pot.

They would turn into machines with hammers and screwdrivers
for hands. I had always wanted to save one from the sink,
learn their little bubble language, dreamt of keeping
it in the bathtub for I had seen a similar scenario in a sitcom.

My mother would actually smile as she salted the water
and made sure everyone knew it was time
to cut the potatoes. I'm trying to accept my mother
has been doing this a long time. Made me hide
the shells, antennae, the evidence in the bushes
and she'd pass the potato salad around, sliced egg,
red paprika. Oh, she had been doing this a long time
trying to bring us all around the table together.

Sea glass

My mother is such a hypochondriac she planned her funeral
in 1989. I remember the playlist. What she wanted:
"I Will Remember You," ok, done, but "Maggie May" by Rod Stewart,
what? I like to ask her about piano, guitar, the fiddle,
but not doctor's notes found explaining tests for a myriad
of reasons due to a blood transfusion she received
in the late '80s. She has never shared the results
or blamed gay people for knowingly spreading HIV
like some people I no longer know. When I go home
I like to clean the bearded vegetables from the crisper,
listen to my mother's advice as *Advocate Extraordinaire
of Solitary Lifestylings*. Since my father's New Year's
Resolution to dissolve blood ties she runs straight
lines on the hospital gym treadmill at night. At least I know
we've had the same scares. We've both been startled
by moose on the lawn. But I want to live
to find out how many prunes is too many prunes, etc.
There is a limit. And I know I am not a person
my mother wanted me to become — I am a beachcomber,
not a fish person. If I was I would be outted
as an out-of-season lobster fisherman.
My mother jokes about taking the neighbour's boat
out, yet no boat exists, just the water under it.
If I was going to share my twenties, my blueberry neck years
it would be the part without myself waiting in clinics
and thinking that as a gay I always need to be tested
to find something wrong in me, even the microscopic,
and if I did take the boat out, I could take my Hans Christian
Andersen out to sea, and read, and floating there maybe
as part of the sky. My mother doesn't have to know
how many men, or how many *Chatelaine* magazines
I have read waiting, thinking about a time in Ottawa

with a lovely Fort Lauderdale single father
who wanted me to join him on his actual living boat
with a propeller, or the coordinates of Venus
to the west which was years ago, and I am here, floating
in Toronto talking about what may have not existed.

Cargo memories

I like to be naked and comfortable with my older friend I treasure it
he likes it at the beach, and who cares if we are naked

I am just realizing this now but we are all chromosomes
at the heart of it. My summer body is my winter

fat glistening. Nothing is ever going to sink how I feel.
Behind my house was the Atlantic, my village made for export

of sawdust, trees. Big cargo boats to take pieces of my town
across the ocean. Time path and least time path.

It feels like the tail end of happy hour when memory leaves
you gauging the multi-phases of life. I remember thinking my body

is a tadpole body in Nova Scotia — itself shaped like a tadpole
body and seeing the ship as a much larger frog splitting open the water

floating like it was Jesus or something much more sinister and now
I text my mother and ask in a more serious adult way about the cargo

ships and what they wanted she said *what cargo ships I'm not sure
what you are talking about because there was also yachts*

and I said sternly *they were cargo ships* and she responds *ok ok
they probably wanted wood chips or pipes or they were picking up*

something at the port. I have a hard time believing in art saving
the world when there are so many holes just in me alone

and there is no Earth-like planet like this Earth-like planet.
I'm guilty thinking of poetry as not being a life

preserver — sometimes it makes me feel good just for a while.
I stare at the head of my beer and think *let me get to the golden stuff*

and the sun touches my face like a mother with a warm washcloth.
My older friend is fine lying in the sand, has been asleep and got a scar

but is sparkling with little minerals, microscopic rocks, who used to be parts
of a larger, bigger, more important life of parts.

View-Master

I have woken up in your chest hair, America, and settled in
to the hotel from the internet. Boyfriend turned away

at the border is coming tomorrow, separate cars. I'm stuck behind
a red Crossfire, hot red, that's trying to bypass the heart

of downtown Portland. I'm way past it all — past Seattle, endless
gambling casinos, the Home-O-Expo, and the religious billboards.

This is America. Think Super-Valu. God is watching. Sometimes
I think we are going too fast. Boyfriend says, *Keep going,*

I'll meet you. I admire the persistence. Car commercials are right.
We want the horsepower, not to get held up. Getaways

can be so flexible! It's out the window that everything stretches:
the Lummi-Nation, old trees, the caterpillar of roadway.

Yellow stripes composed of dashes. The night clerk
says the hotel was a gay bathhouse, a rendezvous point, still

with the original pool. Sometimes I think we're going too fast
into syndication. I take all the garbage from my pockets, mint

wrappers and old directions. I investigate nearby cities. Olympia
and its sacred water source. You'll die there if you drink it

is the myth. Sometimes commitments run that deep. Watch
skate kids do the goofy-foot, get a burrito from the new place.

The next day a rooster congratulates the sun for its return
to his receptive world. Boyfriend is on his way, coming

with nighttime. At Lucky 7 my money gives me away.
I drink the water, drive, get cut off on the shoulder of the road.

I want to drive the Sound, its curves. Pass a man half submerged
fly-fishing in white water, my personal Rockwellian blip

at the turnpike. I think we're going too fast but you want
to cram it all in. Olympic forest, a museum in Sequim

of television, movie, and animal stars. What *is* the hold up?
Where is the ice machine? In a Hamburger Mary's you once

held me so tight I tasted my heart. At the hotel I Google
the internet for Yahoo Answers. *Why do roosters have that*

knee-jerk reaction? Holly in Des Moines says it's to be on top.
She's a real chicken lady. I change. I want to change. In the pool

I believe in gay ghosts. That boyfriends can be banned from
crossing due to way too much self-possession. Nighttime is sprawling,

a convenience store-clerk rings me up, asks me, *Is this it?*
God, I'm thick with existentialism. This is not my field!

Tomorrow I will wake up and fly in a hot-air balloon
tethered to the Earth. I'll visit the museum of famous dogs.

Maurice

You'd sit on that rat-eaten chair in the kitchen
at night writing Rachel and Adulterous Woman better parts.

They'd wear dark oceans of mascara in your hands
& look right streal or prance naked in the forest moonlight

drinking water with a herd of deer. I'd follow your hoof-
prints to Haha on the Hill to visit your folks,

washing your hands in the stream
before you go — and oh, looking back, how your hair caught

the wind and swam like a school of minnows.
After the doughboys go on the stew

you'd sit in your chair, close your eyes to Mozart and sigh.
I know you love Mozart with all your heart. I plant

a burly kiss on your brow. In bed at night
I hear the door click and you prowl the night

till the sky goes periwinkle. Once you came home
from your funkhole whispering *I can speak worm now.*

At night I don't wonder where my love is, if you're hanging Dickinson
poems from the trees in your dringle-way or draining the heel-taps

from the table. You are just unbelievable because one night
I saw you springing over the mountains.

George

Maybe you've heard that I'm a drunk
for George Orwell. Well, I admit
under this tree with the whippoorwills
I am filled by George Orwell. I should work
on my cookery. Cook porridge for George
to gorge his gorgeous mouth on
but I might lose my spot under the pines
with my old George Orwell. What a dream
my poor will makes me dream.

I would peel any number of potatoes
to please him. Under his whip or will
I'd be defenseless (or well, at least kind
of kittenish) and have strange urges
to present him tea that I pour well.
Oolong or Pekoe. Well, I'd climb down
to him if I were Juliet. His Romeo, at least,
would make perfect sense. He'd persuade
me to come down to the Limehouse
and smoke one with him. We'd pull nightshade
from his garden, and I would have to settle
to be with him somehow, in the shade
of this pine with the whippoorwills.

Tool shed

Dad could raise a tool shed, that much is evident,
because he came from strong foundations, with materials
from his father. The ball-headed hammer older than him.
And built in a day, the shed made sensible, practical, and secure
and painted a cow pattern. Perhaps he dreamed of being a cow-
father as I dreamed of being a full-out gay person.
Everything so sensible when it came to wood,
building with nails. A constant on the land his father haunted,
and his father before him, the gardener, who made vodka
with potatoes in a closet made magic by vodka. This gardener,
this relative, who wore his mother's bloomers,
standing knee-high in potatoes, became famous
for his vegetation sense. Adorations and heirlooms in long aisles.
Dad, he had hung an old scythe above the window
and it was his father's eye and eyebrow
so he was always around in some fashion.
Dad of course celebrated the tool shed with Labatt Blue
and a fire for the neighborhood, danced, too just beyond
the bedsheets on the clothesline. Mom then loved him,
the silhouette, the spirits what went to his head.
Dad's tool shed has feet still, but Mom sold his Toyota
and changed the locks good. Put in a tulip
bed. Mom liked how they returned every season,
and she planted carrots for longevity of the eye,
and for their spectacular root systems.

The poem says

Start the poem with a failing metaphor. *Actor carries Metaphor*, the Nightly Mirror reports. Drive the poem down roads and over the green bridge. Tell it your humble beginnings. Tell it your mother's long black hair used to fly behind her when she rode motorcycle to Foodland. Tell it of your body's natural predilection for deceiving. Tell the poem your mother is pointing out the constellation *Monoceros*. To read into that. Tell it you are driving with your mother and you will call later. Tell it that all your triumphs are in need of drastic engineering. Soon all the books will be wet. Tell the poem that. Tell the poem your mother remembers those rooms above the church waiting lonely with the expectation of becoming herself. Tell the poem your mother confuses Franco with Dean. James is such a common name in town, all the Jameses turn around when they hear those letters invisibly tied together. Tell the Jameses it wasn't them, just trips to the grocery store feel heavy loaded. If the poem complains that it is too late. Tell the poem you're waiting for whatever has caught fire in your mother's chest. Tell the poem your mother believes in the old language of piss and vinegar. Tell the poem not to exclaim. Myrtle in your nostrils on your nightly walk, tell the poem that. Tell the poem not to come back if that's what you want. Tell the poem you haven't been to church in some time, that you forget when to kneel. Tell the poem you want to be your mother. The poem holes its way in. The poem says.

Contemporary

The Bell Canada representatives are all here for a conference
called Team Building Weekend. The SkyTrain line is flooded
with them. Who will transfer my emergency calls?

The ticket lady does not care to know how I feel
about this but it's my birthday month. My life brims
on the edges of this platform where we are all told
to expect light at the end of tunnels.

A man bargains with the representatives with *The Sun
Also Rises,* a truly water-damaged text. A bookseller
on bookseller time. This morning I stood up
to the shower. I said, *no, you're out to lunch!*

I would never do the same thing as the other people,
like swallowing water from the sky. It just seems
dangerous not to think for yourself these days.

Sara texts, saying she is floating on the Pacific, and I respond
please watch out for whales they are so temperamental.
She's on a boat which had broken down, says her desire for things
larger than herself has been prolonged for way too much time.
She texts *I'm in a forest of a man's beard* — which has got to be
a metaphor for how close she feels to other people.

I will never understand boats or how they are built
not to sink. I don't want to know. There's better ways to
get around. Once I was buried underground — this was Toronto
transit — nearly two hours. I couldn't complain.
Someone kept yelling this is where we end up anyway

and now I feel like a bird on the SkyTrain. At stops I see tons
of what's going on. Main Street, Science World, the portable gardens
behind the Audi dealership. I see vegetables, little green
promises of tomatoes, Things are built to move. At the bottom
of the stairs, the bookseller asks me for the time
but I just don't have it.

Couch potato

I get so worried when I see space news. I heard astronauts
incinerate their underwear and the ash falls to Earth.

Humans have just dug so much, but in the space continuum
there's probably this ease of quiet. Floating

would take the pressure off my ankles, which Mom has
always described as delicate. I go to libraries a lot

just to focus my escapism. I leave every root behind
when I leave. I am running from problems

of a terribly personal nature. I like finding new life
but my receptors are just so used to balancing the gravity

of this Earth. There are landscapes here I will never see
in my lifetime. I reduce the pain all through the Late Night

line up. I have lived too long beneath my hair. I read shampoo
bottles born from the need to feel sexier. At lunch, a fortune cookie

opened up to me. I am half-way through the honeymoon
rice then it's *Jeopardy* all day. Trebek's ability to navigate

this puzzle board is flat-out inspiring but I don't know why
we get any encouragement. I want to feel intoxicated

with jokes about life but I'll chase my losses and learn to
excuse anything comic and lie in the flowers of my sofa.

Kiss a horse

I dream I lived in a world where you barter with pigs
for medical care. It is Nietzsche's birthday

and people are just butterflying through the used bookstore.
I don't know anything about him except that he really loved

to kiss horses, which is friendly. A man with a comb-
over says to the cashier that Nietzsche book has a convalescence

that will part his hair perfectly. I guess I should buy
some so I can iron out the kinks in my life.

At Starbucks I am about to ask for a restart
on the free internet. Sometimes it is the only place real

to me. I lather myself in repeating. We are living
post-ear. Overheard on the street car was the knowledge

that there are superior and inferior components to life.
That is just way too over my head.

In my neighbourhood I see police on horses. It is summer
and everyone's windows are up. I love you,

I love the orange cranes along the water. We had a good run,
created and made myths and we're always out browsing

for something. It is Nietzsche's birthday. Civilization loves
the classics. I need to go to London

Drugs because I'm in an absence of necessities. Traffic
is crazy. I see myself in sections in the mirror section.

Tree of Mars

I'm told that space is expanding but I don't know
what that means for me personally.

I fall asleep in the Laundromat with puzzles
in my lap. I need a solution for five across. *Home*

of the Albatross? Some of us travel in Walmart-sized
herds. Follow the wet and dry cycles.

Some relax in the gun section and others turn back
to avoid certain death. A psychic once said I have a blue

triangle on my forehead but it wasn't a literal
meaning. I question why we're here and what we're doing.

Solutions for plastic. Cognizant of deficits.
Use and misuse of course I'm aware of it.

I'm experiencing a moral injury. I got my boy
feeling blue. I have taken a blow

to my confidence area. Scientists spend
too much money on moons. Rings on moons

of Saturn. That is what they are all into. The power of love.
How much should I care about trees

on Mars. Curiosity can tell me. I have a great deal
of faith in oracles.

Seussians

We have been working on harvesting
the minerals from other planets. Jade Rabbit, have you

collected your vacation pay? Making the best of a bad
situation is like digging for gold in deep space.

Through study, you might find verbs as useful
and empty. I am taking time off to play peekaboo.

I have my air conditioner set to Soft Country Breeze. Sorry,
am I breathing ok? My dad says to stop worrying

about how things are but I find that things constantly go
missing. When I walk along the sea-

wall true luxury seems timeless. Towers of steel
and aluminum. The Living Shangri-La, Cathedral Place.

I make friends with the F-word. An artist's rendering of the camel
ancestor reveals a desert secret. The fat-filled hump helped it

survive extremes. Don't I recall someone saying the future would hold
concealed truths? I need to decide what is my backup plan.

Once a debt collector said I had better start selling my furniture,
so, as a protagonist I have encountered a few problems.

NASA has the technology to show us worlds we will see
never in our lifetime. We're too focused on the Moon's

resources. The marriage of time and gas. Anxiety mounts.
I know a place in the rocket will be a popularity contest.

Moonshot

In his baseball years, Dad never got home
but he loved to swear and win. Left-
field position of the baseball diamond,
a Rocket. He loved to smoke his opponents
and smoke Players Extra Lights,

drank blue Gatorade for electrolytes.
I preferred the original Blue Jays, had none
of my father's athletic prowess, wore
a large red Converse sweatshirt to hide
my body which Dad had ripped
off me because I looked too much like a fruit,
a tomato, which I had thought he loved
so much. He drank Kokanee with tomato juice
his elixir of youth, made his language loose, Oh,
Dad, driving home nine innings in, oh how you danced
into the land of the living room lamps.

Why I like baseball fields

It was hard to know baseball when all that interested me were the moths
and sometimes big ones.

I loved their team, so disorganized, and from where?

Like masks that folded in on themselves
that flew away.

Dad would run first
maybe make it home

without knowing this: legs like eye-
lashes and special powders
for flying.

They go crazy for little beams of light.
I love them for that still.

How could you go through life not appreciating the mystical
part of night life, or the June bug —

the living acorns of the insect world!

When voices from the crowd rise with the ball I cringe
thinking of being hit

and imagine the voices as little legs
on a light bulb, the fragile glass, their excitement.

Your dad's a regular guy

Your dad's a regular guy, sometimes you imagine
he's not. He was the first to go
belly up at your sister's wedding, blocking the punch
bowl, the antique crystal centerpiece
on a doily of lace. He wore out his dream

suit, sky-blue cool cat number he married in circa
1977. He was a new prairie oil worker
until he caught fire as part of the night
crew, his hands burned leopard, old banana.
Some things burn and some don't
that's what happens in Alberta.

He's a Sheet Harbour Rocket, certified
on fire by the volunteer fire department
and surrounding areas. He's a player, left-
fielder who lost his eye tooth to a Ninja
Turtle action figure. He disappeared in Vegas,
and we forgave him — everyone slips —
it was a lapse, he was absent, came back
with coasters, a lapis lazuli key ring.

He put quarters over your eyes
if you fell asleep on *Hockey Night in Canada*,
I believe you were dead to him, do you remember
him curled on your bedroom floor,
so, you might notice something feline about him,
he only needs you when he wants to be let back in.

Dad with tomato plants

Dad would come to my room at night and water himself
with my secret stash of Coca-Cola.

It made me feel like such an adult that he was coming to me,
all red-faced and flushed like alcohol.

Even though he was the one making the real money
putting tomatoes into cans.

Driving to Stellarton in what I could only understand
as a sense of success at having any job at all

in Nova Scotia. My dad put the tomatoes into the cans
which was like finishing what his father started — oh my god

generational. His father loved himself a big Bulgarian Triumph,
or the big money fruits, the Mortgage Lifters.

I liked the dead mice, their sweet tiny eyes and how they
just wanted their family to be fed and happy.

Crap, I am not a farmer yet I liked the wild rhubarb, calendula,
herbs, and greenhouse flowers. The beauty of an African violet.

Dad turned into a tomato plant every morning
after a heavy night of buying Coca-Cola from me

leaving behind dimes and nickels
in the morning like some sort of fairy.

Potato People

On my father's side were the potato people, gardens they had.
Roses, potatoes, and cabbages you couldn't get anywhere else.
Potatoes had beds as big as Olympic swimming pools
I once swam through and laid in exhausted from growing
up. I think they were liked for they were reliable,
you just let them go.

The first time my childhood actions had consequences was me standing up
in the kitchen wondering what would happen to me for swimming
for now there were grandfather tensions.

Now I take a hard stand on vegetable life. I loved to go
beep beep in my car imagining myself a real adult overseeing an orchard
of potatoes. I liked to stand on the edges looking at signs of life.

We fed the pigs the potatoes that did not survive my Olympic dream.
I began to see gardens meant death. Squash
and tomato beds were set with traps checked each morning for mice,
a thing I developed a love for from television.

As potato and garden people, mice were enemies and farm cat food.
Oh my god everything is linked in a circle. I hated that mice
had to die for vegetables to live.

This was one of my first meetings with death. It is why I cannot eat
salad. When we would take the fancier vegetables to rich tourists,

they ate radishes and cucumber unknowingly implicated in murder.
But potatoes, they are not blind. They know what is going on down
there. I dream they whisper, touch the mouse's whiskers, say,
you better get out of here, get running.

Potatoes in my life

Kindergarten teachers are the first to break the news
that potatoes undergo a lot of changes.

Mrs. Gardener didn't have to tell me that, I knew it,
lived it.

Could never sleep without a light
I'd wake up screaming.

I put one on the windowsill, my mother throws
fifty-pound bags over her shoulders
like He-Man.

Put one in the cupboard and it grew hair
like my grandmother's.

After my grandfather died we had to buy
them and it was pitiful for the community.

He would wait all summer to see potatoes;
I mean this was his life,

and kill anything that messed with them
to which I silently disagreed.

I spent a lot of time by myself in the wild,
and made my own house

because I believed a garden is a community
of living things that don't talk to communicate,

yet I named snails and educated them
on dead nettle, friend to the potato.

I loved the cupboard potato, it came out neglected.
Long, thin arms that said *hold me, my arms are empty.*

Inheritance and one ghost

As adults, brother tried to convince us he wanted the fiddle
and violin to learn how to play it: *where was it now?*

We all knew he wanted to sell it. All the music had left
the family when the radio was invented.

No one wanted the sewing
machine and downstairs, the antique furniture

Dad was literally burning in the backyard, Jesus he was such a flamer.
I loved to go through the things, trinkets, and crap

in my grandmother's sewing machine for it proved who lied
about the past. All the very old buttons from the clothing

of relatives, a hat box with the name *Martina* written on the top,
and the curled-up Polaroid pictures of all my grandfather's

brothers, and Cyril again, who pops up in little hand-
written notes about his singing voice. And all the jewels,

fake but jewels, and one real gold coin, kept in a wedding ring box,
a modern-day electric bill, and medals from wartime,

which I think made people no longer want anything
to do with music because there was no voice after that,

a suitcase filled with old sheet music, and a well-preserved moth,
and, and another medal, star-shaped with a blue ribbon

not for growing vegetables as it looked too official, and a notebook
of recipes written out in longhand in my grandmother's voice

now pulled from this green Steno spiral notebook. I hate duplicating
a grandmother recipe. When she died we inherited the egg beaters,

her dried psalms, the testament, spice rack, knick-knacks, her horse
plates. No one understood her recipe language so in death she came out

of the Steno yet I still wanted something more tangible. Still,
in her flowered blouse she said *I want you to be the holiday fruitcake*

guy. Being haunted kind of sucks but you have to laugh
at the fact your brother's learning the fiddle, the violin —

but he just wanted something to keep. I told my grandmother we gutted
her house of her belongings, the envelope of my mother's baby hairs,

we were alone in the kitchen, laughing at the peeled potatoes, now eyeless,
they reminded her of the bald heads of all beautiful and dead uncles.

Life of Bryan

My father is such a liar sometimes that he forgets his life
and I have no idea what is real, who my great-grandmother as a person
was, aside from boys were boys and girls
girls. I had an uncle in Red Deer with a family cut up by divorce
and I have met only once, this uncle, Bryan, who I believed
committed suicide by hanging and — like me — was a Cancer
with ruby gemstones. But it is funny

what is recalled at parties with too much alcohol, that he was not a ghost,
and lived divorced in Alberta as a gay person.
When I lived in Alberta six months I didn't hide my queer side
and didn't think anything
about the homophobia which I believed to be a present
aspect of living. I became addicted to cucumber water, tried to straighten
up my life in the sense of saving something
in the way of money. I feel like my dad made me complicit
in burying my uncle alive.

When I asked yesterday, years later, how Bryan had died
he was quick to text back *heart attack, why?*
Oh, but *I thought you said he committed suicide because he was gay*

I had interior-decorated poems with metaphors hanging
all over them, was told simply by straight peers *stick to the fluffy
topics.* Like Drag Brunch recaps, or?
To be unclear about death or the fact that Bryan was alive
when he was dead, well, I know how that is. It is certainly not fluffy
like scrambled eggs at a Drag Brunch.

Can love for someone really disappear because they are gay, queer?
When I was interrogated about my sexuality I said *ummm bye*
I said *ummm bye* but I was not going anywhere
and everyone was confused but me.

Imagine just forgetting about someone 'cause they called you out
to the telephone to share an honesty. My friend Amanda
owned a large print of Dali's *Metamorphosis of Narcissus* and I heard them,
what they were saying about holding up your own egg.

Owen, a pixie-cut boy who thought like me and lived
quietly on the living room floor. We all said *I love you* when he died
on Nintendo, and I loved when he turned my belly into a pillow
and listened to the Zelda music. We made sure to love every moment
the only gospel-type thing I still hear. Oh, my uncle, his heart,
the distance he went, the telephone cord wrapped around his finger.

More details forthcoming

Now even still I am hesitant to ask about my uncle Bryan,
not Brian, the Uncle with Webbed Toes, no.
I had fallen early in love with my own reflection
in a driveway puddle.
I want to know if he fell
in love. I am still trying to love myself.
I have three memories of Bryan, none I was present
for, so they are my father's memories you see
how hard it is to get the real truth
how hard it is to admit when you aren't to question a claustrophobic place
a house with several closets
your parents expect you to leave

never. I have asked myself to take a lot into this poem
which no one may read. Dad said Bryan is like me,
the elder brother. What I remembered from the night the phone rang
was *Hockey Night in Canada*, and Don Cherry in pink plaid,
and Dad pretending to throw up or to be choking on a sunflower
seed that his elder brother was gay.
Bryan called and said he was coming out
which is simply brave in Northern Alberta
where I ended up living once in February
and was driven to the outskirts after admitting I was gay
to a co-worker only to be brought back eventually to town.
I forget how the story went.
Dad had thought at first flying, he was flying from Red Deer
to Sheet Harbour but no,
Dad had come back into the room of the living
knowing *coming out* is a loaded term. He spit that his brother was gay,
that *Bryan's a faggot*
and from then on I watched *The Kids in the Hall* very carefully,
admitted nothing honestly, covered myself, wore pants everywhere.
No one would see my body and know.

Because I felt very gay at twelve. I would mow the lawn and see half of me
in the basement windows and what a chicken
I would have to become, fluffy feathers, thinking wow, look
how your life can disappear when you admit feelings.
I was still young, figuring out my body and knowing absolutely
nothing about puberty or pubic hair for real,
it became my Easter surprise. No one talked about the body.
How we could change.
For my father I closed off all my windows, germinated in my room
a few weeks but I kept hearing Bryan reaching out like a science
potato in a dark cupboard — when everyone was scared of HIV
and kissing, scared of the telephone
coin return slots he kept reaching out.
Dad tried to kill his brother with his mind.
I can't call or text. The telephone is mysterious.
On the other end could be your uncle opening up
a portal to what could have been his very real life.

The men in my family never talk about Alberta

Coming into Alberta the highway is lined with sneakers
from the past adventurers. Markers of feet going on forever.
A waitress in a railway café asks do I want to sit in Saskatchewan
or Alberta? I order roast beef and sit by retired train tracks.
My father came to Alberta lonely to work for oil, a detail
from letters he wrote my mother. He called himself
a traveller, amateur coin collector. Found pesos from
Oaxaca. He called the prairies the tropics — so different
from his birth in the salt and rain and being born
inside a fish, as far as personal myths go.

The men in my family come to Alberta. I stayed
for six months working in Slave Lake. I had to plug
myself in so I did not freeze solid. My uncle grew
four kids never heard from again. All I know of my uncle
was in my father's words — that he died
because he was gay, no more explanations.
I wrote my uncle once
but there was no response from his house.
I had no idea what he did to live. My father
did a full nine months out there playing oilman,
then boomeranged back, fully rejuvenated.

When I got to Edmonton it was nice and weird.
Carpeted light rail transit with chandelier.
I let a man kiss me in the bookstore.
He gave me the vibes. I wanted to leave
my sneakers in the slim erotica section.
He asked me to come to the Best Ass Contest
over coffees. His had a bullet wound in it.
He would not beat me, he promised.

I told him I had already won. I treated myself
to the Best Western. I remembered from baseball
years the bacon was real good. My brother is now
a very different man. A man gave him a new nose
but now he can now afford a new nose. At the railway
café I had wondered how close I was to the border —
if I should've ate my sandwich in Saskatchewan
while I could, extended a little, my roots.

Live-in boyfriend

Wow, this brand-new landscape and gay officially
in the soil of your bedroom. I raise one arm like a student
maybe of real love
then the other, long pale tubulars. A second
generation farmer I find a little of myself
staring into this painting of yours
the stream in it, stare into the hidden face of a girl
washing her hair
that even you had not discovered till I pointed with my arms,
my real arms.

I love to unravel in the morning like a fighting fish, fins
pink and blue like kindergarten names.
I always always always wanted more colours
never the pink and blue of gender reveals.

The streets are full of just school kids swimming
and sounds of living
the birds in a musical, a man who has kicked a can —
I can open the blind for the real scenery.

The maple trees of Oakwood perfect in their birthday suits.
The street where a chip bag thinks it can fly.

The undiscovered woman in your painting she is taken
in by her reflection, the flow of water. I don't know.

Does it take a while to figure out who to blame
because I'm afraid to admit when something matters?

The living room plants get the benefits from the outside world,
why not us a little more?

You mist them every morning, peel a gas station Sunkist
all in one go. You are immersed in the environmental section
of the Metro, not even a real newspaper, yet you plow through.
I am aware the water comes down, recycles. The plants that do this.
I feel you on water treatment.

I am standing here full bladder. Smell orange, alive as flowers.
How much water, how much have you lost? I smoke my Pall Malls
out the window. I drink water from the tap.

If your dad is like Homer

Then he hasn't stopped talking to you all these years
that in a past life he had a long narrative

arc that he was a player
of baseball

Your mother found pictures of him
in different families buried in mittens

He ran the diamond home

"Travels for work a lot" to "places"
Sudbury, Wine Country, Erin

He calls magazines books and loves a lot
stories about himself —

about himself from afar — Lowville,
Greater Napanee, Lindsay,

He has a mean punch and borrows
the Odyssey

to make donuts in his old high-school field
and battled the Great Male Pattern Baldness

and tries to make you feel good
about your evil general
hairiness but you're still wearing pants
in the water?

and throws you in the water
full pants

to see whether it is crucial
or beneficial to male development

and digs you out of the sand
when you have transformed into the gorgeousness
which is mermaid

and he is way out in left field
a speck a seed
about how you feel in this goddamned
journey into your own body.

For my future wilderness

I am forgetting what is seen in the bathroom mirror,
what is on my passport, my license for the Land

Rover. I'm over being real and maybe I'll love me.
Yes, I am scared of news but that fear is my shit

and my Land Rover is my set of feet, and I claim to be
a farmer/botanist type yet the only plant to withstand

my intense love is the aloe vera, the cat of the plant world
who wants nothing from me it seems.

I take my dreams as true. I see the ghosts of cats and I take my dreams
as true. I begin to take out my face, hey here it is, and identify

parts of the forest I would like to label kin. Dandelion lichen fir moss
and their slow languages all around me in High Park where I sing

Whitney Houston and come to terms with middle-age and ideas like:
that if something was going to happen it would have already.

I don't care what people say about me personally anymore, I found
my own mouth which speaks for me

and when I invited a Grindr guy over I confidently ripped my shirt
off like in porns and when he frowned at my appendix scar

disappointed that I had once almost died I said: *no, it's not a scar
it's my second mouth telling you to get out of my house.*

I just have now, certain beliefs. In Kindergarten, months before power
was lost, I met a boa constrictor, named Margaret, doing and undoing

in the zoo-man's hands, oh, and I ran and ran
my fingers over its scales, so close to celebrity, and afraid

perhaps to touch an actual Bible character before it disappeared
with the zoo-man through the foliage of children's drawings

hanging like mirrors, complete with our versions of the world
and all the people, the tiny animals, a kingdom of sunflower, lilacs

in bloom, and horseshoe sitting arrangements so we saw people
as people and in the future would not cut down their goodness.

When I see trees frowning it makes me unhappy. I get it,
they have seen everything and science may find the information

in tree rings, or a rock thrown into a deep lake, nature's voice
recording. I am sitting at home, slowing down

to find places where animals will eat out of my hands, I love
how it tickles and it's, like, two kinds of nourishment.

It is like receiving counsel and peace. Google Earth and see things
connected like veins, the blue highways, the light

blue lake, where I can totally get down
and hold my head over its brim, drinking and drinking in

and this is my animal pose, this is the look for me, it's animal
and I ask what is up do you have a manual on how to behave

and I am all fours, asking not to be or not be. But —
I can be this poem. I can be wilderness.

Thank you to *Matrix*, the *Matador Review*, *Bywords*, the *Malahat Review*, *Poetry Is Dead*, *Arc Poetry Magazine*, *Qwerty*, the *Rusty Toque*, *Geist*, and anyone else for publishing earlier versions of these poems, thank you so much for seeing something in the poems. Most of these poems were written in Vancouver, on the unceded traditional territory of the Musqueam, Squamish, and Tsleil-Waututh Nations.

Thank you to Sheryda Warrener for pulling me out of the dirt and for her guidance.

Thank you to Linda Svendsen, Rhea Tregebov, Ian Williams, Kayla Czaga, Ken Babstock, Karen Solie, Chelene Knight, and Keith Maillard for their support and kindness, their eyes and patience while I wrote this book.

Thank you to CAConrad who inspired the title of the last poem.

Thank you also, so much, to my undergraduate creative writing teachers who made this book possible. Rishma Dunlop, David Goldstein, and Priscila Uppal have helped me in ways I only realized after the fact and am still realizing today. I will always remember you.

Matthew Walsh hails from the Eastern Shore of Nova Scotia and has twice travelled by bus across Canada. Their poems and short fiction have appeared in *Joyland, Matrix, Arc Poetry*, the *Malahat Review, HOAX, Existere*, the *Rusty Toque, Qwerty*, the *Capra Review*, the *Matador Review, Poetry Is Dead*, and *Geist*, as well as the anthology *Writing the Common*. They were named *Geist*'s Emerging Poet of the Month in October 2012, received York University's Poetry Award in 2013, and won the John Newlove Poetry Award in 2014. Walsh holds an MFA from the University of British Columbia and lives in what is now called Toronto.

Photo: Raffy Ochoa